ESSAY WRITING
THE SECRETS REVEALED

Cindy M.

PARTRIDGE
A Penguin Random House Company

REFERENCE & PRACTICE

FOR BEGINNERS &

INTERMEDIATE

STUDENTS OF ESL

ISBN: Softcover   978-1-4828-9872-9
             eBook   978-1-4828-9874-3

To order additional copies of this book, contact
Toll Free 800 101 2657 (Singapore)
Toll Free 1 800 81 7340 (Malaysia)
orders.singapore@partridgepublishing.com

www.partridgepublishing.com/singapore

CONTENT

NOTE FROM THE AUTHOR

If you have bought this book, let me personally congratulate you for making a wise decision and a worthy business investment. **I say wise because if you are a student, you are on your way to getting better grades, and if you are a teacher or tutor, you can expect instant improvement in the overall student performance and grade or an increase in the number of students.**

Throughout my study years, writing essays had always been a struggle. I've always had trouble coming up with ideas, and completing an essay within a given time frame was often a nightmare particularly in examinations. Even when I did complete the essays, they were never short of mistakes. I know for a fact that there are still many who share the same problems.

Of course, there has always been a format for essay writing and there are a number of good books offering extensive writing tips and/or essay samples. However, most only cover the format and writing styles with little emphasis on factors contributing to mistakes habitually made when writing. Reading essay samples is good for written variety and enhancing vocabulary but it also often encourages students, especially those studying English as a second language, to copy and memorise the samples, thus leading to plagiarism.

Fortunately when I was teaching in Singapore, I discovered **the secrets to writing commendable argumentative and factual essays,** which **significantly help reduce mistakes and hence boost confidence.** As a conscientious teacher, I knew my students would have the same problems I had. So I decided to do research in the hope of finding an explanation that they would understand. Many are not aware that the secrets are in fact hidden formulas.

I remember my writing improved after studying a book on how to prepare assignments but it only had one part of the formula. Through my teaching experience and readings, I managed to extract, conclude and simplify the formulas. I have successfully explained them to thousands of students. With God's blessings, the improvements are obvious. I get a lot of OH and AHs whenever I explain the formulas. The responses are proof of how they work for high school, college and university students.

In all honesty, I cannot guarantee that students will score 100 as opinions differ, but I can promise that if the formulas are applied, teachers and students will realize an obvious improvement.

This book is a reference and practice book (workbook) for teachers and students who are teaching and learning English as a second language (ESL). It does not only cover all the essential components necessary for writing good essays, but it also redefines and further explains essay writing rules and necessary terminologies, and it is written in a way that most students of ESL will understand but not necessarily the way it should be taught.

To fully appreciate the value of this book, I recommend that teachers and students start from **The Fundamentals** even though the topics covered may seem easy and repetitive. It is the assumption of prior knowledge that results in the reduction of marks. You will be surprised that even those who presumably have a good grasp of English, make mistakes, and worse, they often go out of topic! **If you want instant improvement, you must study or review the fundamentals!**

I have also written a chapter on summary writing. It, of course, comes with a formula that has helped many students with difficulties in rephrasing information. It is an essential topic for tertiary students doing research.

Before expecting improvements, expect mistakes as habits die hard. Many students of ESL whom I have taught have this writing style that is very much dictated by a direct translation from their mother tongue and broken English. Understanding and applying are separate matters. They may understand the formulas but as with many forgetful and careless learners, many neglect to apply the skills learnt. Similar to understanding any mathematics formula, practice makes perfect and the good news is that it will not take long for beginner and intermediate students to master writing coherent essays.

Once the formulas are understood and applied, teachers and students will see instant improvements in the following aspects of writing: **sentence structure**, **tense application**, **vocabulary use**, **expression**, **coherency**, **writing speed and more!**

Teaching the formulas has been a blast because I get to see students realizing their own mistakes and editing their own work independently all within a short period. It is a dream coming true.

I wrote this book many years ago and have copied the exercises and distributed them. Publishing was not my priority until I realized I had photocopied thousands, and with the information given by Trafford's publishing consultant on copyright issues, this book is finally in print.

ACKNOWLEGDEMENTS

- To GOD for blessing me
- To my family for guiding and supporting me
- To my friend and teacher, Colin D'Souza for being kind and patient

Thank you!
May God continue to bless all of you!

CHAPTER 1

ESSAY WRITING
THE
FUNDAMENTALS

Fewer Mistakes, Greater Confidence!

Before learning how to write an essay, it is essential to first master three basic components:

1. Basic Sentence Structure,
2. The Simple Tenses, and
3. Words and Phrases to Avoid

ⅭⅭⅭⅭⅭⅭⅭⅭⅭⅭⅭⅭⅭⅭⅭⅭⅭⅭⅭ

THE BASIC SENTENCE STRUCTURE

Many teachers assume students studying English as a second language are familiar with or have mastered the structure. Likewise many of these students take the basic sentence structure for granted. Unfortunately, that is one assumption and neglect which cost marks. Writing a coherent essay is very much dependent on correct sentence structure. So here is a basic explanation.

Must remember!

A complete sentence must have at least one subject and one verb.

1 subject	+	1 Verb	=	A complete sentence
Clowns	+	entertain	=	*Clowns entertain.*
She	+	writes	=	*She writes.*
The assertive coach	+	shouts	=	*The assertive coach shouts.*

Must remember!

Each subject and each verb are divided into three categories respectively which create a variation in sentences.

Must remember!

A subject is divided into three parts: **noun, pronoun** and **noun phrase.**

1) Noun

A noun is a general name for a person, an animal, a thing or a place.

Person	Animal	Thing	Place
a politician	an ostrich	a calculator	a café

2) Pronoun

A pronoun is a word which replaces a noun or a noun phrase. i.e. **they, we, you, he, she** and **it**.

Politicians / A politician	An ostrich / A calculator / A cafe
They/ We / He / She	It

3) Noun Phrase

A noun phrase comprises an article, one or more adjectives and a noun.

An article	+	adjective(s)	+	a noun	=	A noun phrase
A	+	silver	+	ring	=	A silver ring
An	+	honest	+	vendor	=	An honest vendor
The	+	rich young	+	socialite	=	The rich young socialite

Write three examples for each of the following noun category. An example has been done for you. Quite a number of students of ESL have lower than average vocabulary knowledge compared to an English speaker. So learn to write beyond the simple and common nouns like pencil, teacher, cat and classroom.

Nouns

Animal	Ostrich	Walrus	Platypus
Person			
Thing			
Place			

Noun Phrase

Write three examples of a noun phrase. An example has been done for you. Again, learn to write beyond the simple and common adjectives like cute, big, and happy. Take up the courage to write more than one adjective.

Must remember!

There is a sequence to writing adjectives. Refer to the following table.

Number	Quality / Characteristics	Size	Shape	Age	Colour	Origin	Noun
three	expensive	small	round	new	gold	German	watches

Example: *A selfish ignorant ghost writer*

1. _____

2. _____

3. _____

Must remember!

A verb is also divided into three parts: **main verb**, **action verb** and **non-action verb.**

1) Main Verb

The main verb refers to the infinitive verb **to be**.

Main Verb	is / am / are / was / were

2) Action Verb

An action verb is a word which generally represents an action.

Action Verb	snatch / wink / yawn

3) A non-action verb

A non-action verb is a word which does not represent an action.

Non-Action Verb	accept / think / acknowledge

Must remember!

Generally, a sentence should have one subject and one verb for it to be complete. Avoid adding or combining more than one category from each component. Note the examples given.

1 subject	+	1 Verb	=	A complete sentence
Noun	+	**Main Verb**	=	**Soldiers are** unsung heroes.
Pronoun	+	**Action Verb**	=	**He lifts** weights.
Noun phrase	+	**Non – Action Verb**	=	**The young graduates think** a lot.

Write three examples for each of the following verb category. Examples are written for you. Similar to the previous practices, write beyond the simple and common verbs like walk, sing and dream.

Action Verbs	scribble	tread	prance
Non-Action Verbs	assent	crave	fancy

Identifying a complete sentence

Indicate whether the following sentences are complete or incomplete. Remember the general rule that a complete sentence must have at least one subject and one verb.

Must remember!

However, there is an exception. A subject is not necessary when giving instructions or orders. For example, it is not necessary to include the name of the person when instructing him to sit down.

Sit down! (Acceptable)   *Anthony, sit down!* (The subject is not necessary.)

Sentences	Complete / Incomplete
Cooking a new dish.	
Is easy.	
A vacation will do you a lot of good.	
Sky surfing very exciting.	

I will take.	
Think about your past.	
Lots of bubbles.	
Abel speaks more than one language.	
She often gets irritated.	
Changing a habit can be frustrating.	
Citizens from every state.	
To get greater benefit from the government	
The differences between young and old.	
The prime minister can speak in public.	
You will perform.	

COMPLEMENT AND MODIFIER   NOTES

Writing one subject and one verb are insufficient for a sentence in an essay. Generally, longer sentences are required. Thus, complements and modifiers are added.

Subject + verb + complement + modifier

COMPLEMENT

Must remember!

A complement is the same as a subject. The difference is it is written after the verb and it answers the questions: **who** and **what**.

subject	+	verb	+	complement
Doctors	+	treat	+	patients (who?)
He	+	lifts	+	weights (what?)

MODIFIER

Must remember!

A modifier answers the questions: **how**, **where** and **when**.

subject	+	verb	+	complement	+	Modifier
Doctors	+	treat	+	patients	+	**unwearyingly (how)** **in clinics and hospitals (where)** **every day (when).**
He	+	lifts	+	weights	+	**persistently (how)** **at the gym (where** **on weekends (when).**

Must remember!

It is not necessary to write all three modifiers in a sentence. Note the examples given.

- Doctors treat patients **every day.**
- He lifts weights at the **gym.**

SENTENCE STRUCTURE   PRACTICE

Rearranging the structure

These are typical incorrect sentences written by students of ESL. Rearrange them according to the correct structure.

1. Drives her car she with speed.

    _____

2. The supermarket I often go to.

    _____

3. She money paid too much.

    _____

4. The Chinese new student has with personal some problems.

    _____

5. It often difficult is to understand Scottish.

    _____

6. The emcee English very fast spoke.

    _____

7. Korean or Japanese food you do prefer?

    _____

8. Sweet talking he very is at good!

    _____

9. Aubrey never I have met.

    _____

10. The principal or you are the teacher?

    _____

THE SIMPLE TENSES

Many do not realize that 90 to 100 percent of the time, the main tense applied in argumentative and factual essays is either simple present or simple past. The reason is simple. Both tenses serve to explain facts, present or past. Let's review the following factual passages. The first passage is written in the simple present and the second is written in the simple past.

SIMPLE PRESENT

FACEBOOK

Facebook is a free social utility which is popular with many internet users. The utility is opened to almost anyone with internet access. There are no membership and entrance fees needed to open an account. Needless to say, similar to free emails, Facebook attracts millions of users worldwide. There are also no admission limitations based on class, gender and profession. Although there is a minimum age requirement, many are able to bluff their way to opening an account.

SIMPLE PAST

THE SEPTEMBER 11 ATTACKS

The September 11 attacks were a series of organized terrorist attacks launched upon the United States on 11th September 2011. Four airliners were hijacked and flown into buildings in New York state and Washington, D.C. Two of the planes crashed into the twin towers of the World Trade Center in New York City which unfortunately caused them to collapse. The third plane crashed into Pentagon which led to the partial collapse of its west wing. And the fourth plane crashed into a field near Pennsylvania after its passengers tried to overcome the hijackers. The number of casualties was more than two thousand.

So for now, it is safe to apply only either the simple present or the simple past without the need to add the continuous, future and perfect tenses. However, if you have not mastered the simple present and past tenses yet, a brief overview of the tenses is written on the following pages.

Must remember!

Subject	+	Verb (s/es)
Noun / Pronoun / Noun Phrase	+	Main / Action / Non Action
Facebook	+	is ...
They	+	control ...
The angry crowd	+	marches

Must remember!

Many students of ESL neglect to acknowledge the importance of singular and plural nouns and how they affect the verbs that follow, thus resulting in mistakes in subject-verb agreement.

Plural Noun	+	Infinitive verb
Rumour **mongers**	+	*spread* baseless statements

Singular Noun	+	verb which ends with s/es
A rumour monger	+	*spreads* baseless statements

Examine how the following passage is written:

Facebook is a free social utility which **is** popular with many internet users. **The utility is opened** to almost anyone with internet access. **There are** no membership and entrance fee needed to open an account. Needless to say, similar to free emails, **Facebook attracts** millions of users worldwide. **There are** also no admission limitations based on class, gender and profession. Although **there is** a minimum age requirement, **many are able** to bluff their way to opening an account.

Subject	Verb
Facebook	is
The utility	is opened (*passive verb form*)
There	are
Facebook	attracts
There	are
there	is
many	are able

ACTIVE OR PASSIVE VERB FORMS NOTES

Sentences can be active or passive.

Active Verb Forms

In active sentences, the thing doing the action is the subject and the thing receiving the action is the complement also known as the object. Most sentences are active.

Subject doing action (SDA) + verb (V) + complement receiving action (CRA)

SDA	+	V	+	CRA
Mechanics	+	repair	+	cars
Michael	+	observes	+	the salesman

Passive Verb Forms

In passive sentences, the thing receiving the action is the subject and the thing doing the action is optionally included near the end of the sentence. Use the passive form if the thing receiving the action is more important or should be emphasized. The passive form is also applied when the subject doing the action is unknown or when you do not want to mention who is doing the action.

Complement receiving action (CRA) + be + past participle of verb (PP) + by + subject doing action (SDA)

CRA	+	be	+	PP	+	by	+	SDA
Cars	+	are	+	repaired	+	by	+	mechanics
The saleman	+	is	+	observed	+	by	+	Michael

PRACTICE

Write three sentences in the active voice and three sentences in the passive voice.

Active Verb Forms

Subject doing action (SDA) + verb (V) + complement receiving action (CRA)

1. _____

2. _____

3. _____

Passive Verb Forms

Complement receiving action (CRA) + be + past participle of verb (PP) + by + subject doing action (SDA)

1. _____

2. _____

3. _____

Write a 150 to 200-word factual passage in the simple present. Choose one of the following topics: *Money, Recycling, Effective Communication, Stress, Earth Hour* or *Globalization.*

TOPIC: _____

_____

_____

_____

_____

_____

_____

_____

_____

_____

_____

_____

_____

_____

_____

_____

_____

_____

_____

_____

_____

_____

_____

PRACTICE 2

Most students neglect to apply the correct tense, and they make habitual mistakes. So here's another practice. Write a 150 to 200-word factual passage in the simple present. Choose another topic besides the one chosen in practice 1: *Money, Recycling, Effective Communication, Stress, Earth Hour* or *Globalization.*

TOPIC: _____

_____ _____

_____

_____

_____

_____

_____

_____

_____

_____

_____

_____

_____

_____

_____

_____

_____

_____

_____

_____

_____

_____

PRACTICE 3

You should realise a significant improvement by now. Just to make sure, this is the final practice for this topic. Write a 150 to 200-word factual passage in the simple present. Choose another topic besides the ones chosen in practice 1 and 2: *Money, Recycling, Effective Communication, Stress, Earth Hour* or *Globalization.*

TOPIC: _____

_____

_____

_____

_____

_____

_____

_____

_____

_____

_____

_____

_____

_____

_____

_____

_____

_____

_____

_____

Must remember!

Subject	+	Regular (d/ed) / Irregular verb (take – took)
Terrorists	+	*attacked* ... (attack)
The crash	+	*led* to ... (lead)

Must remember!

Many tend to forget to change the base form of the verbs to regular and irregular verbs, and this increases the number of unnecessary mistakes.

INCORRECT	CORRECT
They *unload* the goods *yesterday.*	They *unloaded* the goods *yesterday.*
He *eat* three pancakes *this morning*.	He *ate* three pancakes *this morning*.

Examine how the following passage is written:

The September 11 attacks were a series of organised terrorist attacks launched upon the United States on 11th September 2011. **Four airliners were hijacked** and **flown** into buildings in New York state and Washington, D.C. **Two of the planes crashed** into the twin towers of the World Trade Center in New York City **which** unfortunately **caused** them to collapse. **The third plane crashed** into Pentagon which led to the partial collapse of its west wing. And **the fourth plane crashed** into a field near Pennsylvania after **its passengers tried** to overcome the hijackers. **The number of casualties was** more than two thousand.

Subject	Regular (d/ed) / Irregular verb (take – took)
The September 11 attacks	were
Four airlines	were hijacked … flown (passive verb form)
There	are
Facebook	attracts
There	are
there	is
many	are able

Write a 150 to 200-word factual passage in the simple past. Choose one of the following topics: *A late family member*, *The typewriter*, *A celebrity of the 70s, 80s or 90s*, *A classic movie*, *A significant event in history* or *Extinct Animals*.

TOPIC: _____

_____

_____

_____

_____

_____

_____

_____

_____

_____

_____

_____

_____

_____

_____

_____

_____

_____

_____

_____

_____

_____

_____

Again, most students of ESL neglect to apply the correct tense, and they make habitual mistakes. So here's another practice. Write a 150 to 200-word factual passage in the simple past. Choose another topic besides the one chosen in Practice 1: *A late family member*, *The typewriter*, *A celebrity of the 70s, 80s or 90s*, *A classic movie*, *A significant event in history* or *Extinct Animals*.

TOPIC: _____

_____

_____

_____

_____

_____

_____

_____

_____

_____

_____

_____

_____

_____

_____

_____

_____

_____

_____

_____

PRACTICE 3

You should realize a significant improvement by now. Just to make sure, this is the final practice for this topic. Write a 150 to 200 word factual passage in the simple past. Choose another topic besides the ones chosen in Practice 1 and 2: *A late family member*, *The typewriter, A celebrity of the 70s, 80s or 90s, A classic movie, A significant event in history* or *Extinct Animals.*

TOPIC: _____

_____

_____

_____

_____

_____

_____

_____

_____

_____

_____

_____

_____

_____

_____

_____

_____

_____

_____

_____

_____

WORDS AND PHRASES TO AVOID

During my years of teaching, I have noticed a number of misused and overused or unnecessary words and phrases typically written by South East Asian students. These words and phrases are often the outcome of direct translation from their first language. The following is a list of them with explanation to why they should be avoided. I use the word 'avoid' because not all are mistakes but when one reads a good essay or an article in a magazine or journal, these words and phrases are rarely used. Once you learn to exclude these words and phrases, expect instant improvement in your writing.

Must remember!

Words & Phrases to avoid	Reasons for avoiding
People	The word is too general to refer to a specific group. It is often better to use a specific noun to refer to a specific group of people i.e. engineers, entrepreneurs, criminals, etc. But in case the general public is referred, then *many, the majority, most, some* and *a few* are appropriate.
In this world, planet, earth / globe & life	Unless you are studying extraterrestrial beings and are a ghost hunter writing a report, most factual essays involve or talk about people in this world. *World, planet, earth, globe* and *life* are obvious and unnecessary.
Always	The word indicates a 'no miss' situation. For example, say that I tell you I always go to the washroom in my office. Thus, *always* implies that even when it is midnight and I am at home and I need to relief myself, I would drive to my office and use the washroom there, simply because I do not and never miss going to the same washroom. So unless you are very sure, then substitute **always**

	with **often**, **generally**, **sometimes**, **usually**, **normally**, or **occasionally**.
Beside, Besides & Besides that	*Beside* is often confused with *besides*. *Beside* without the 's' means *next to,* and *besides* means *in addition to.* *Besides* and *besides that* are commonly used in conversations. They should be substituted with *furthermore*, *moreover*, *in addition* and *and*.
Have / has	In Chinese and Malay, *have* and *has* mean *in existence* or *available* but in English, they mean *to own* or *to enjoy*. **Have** or **has** are often used with people. If you mean to write in existence or available, use the phrase **there are** or **there is**. Note the examples given. Example 1: • *There have* three books on the table ✗ • *There are* three books on the table ✓ Example 2: • *The table has* three books. (*The books do not belong to the table nor is it owned by the table*) ✗ • *She has* three books placed on the table (*She owns the three books*) ✓
Can	*Can* is a favourite word used to replace *yes*. Note the example given. • **Can you do me a favour?**　　**Can (yes).** It is also often misused in essays. **Can** means *able to* and usually there is a choice to it. Note the difference in meaning. • Fire *kills*. (It's a fact)　　　　　　✓ • Fire *can kill*. (*Imagine that you put your hand on top of a heap of burning wood, do you think the fire has a choice not to burn?*)　　　　✗ Both sentences are grammatically correct but the latter is illogical.

Must	*Must* offers no choice. Do it or otherwise. Note the following example. • **Question:** What should students do to pass a test? **Typical Answer:** They *must* revise. *(What about those students who didn't revise and still pass the test?)* The answer should be 'They *should* revise'.
Will	*Will* is the future tense which indicates an unplanned future. It is rarely used in argumentative and factual essays.
On the other hand	The phrase means **on the contrary** or **however**, but many misinterpret it as **in addition to**.
Thing, something & anything	These words are not specific in meaning or reference. Note the example given. • He does his *thing*. *(Formal writing requires specifications and not something general)*
Everyone / Everybody	This is not a mistake but it is an assumption by many that makes it a mistake. Note the following example:- • *Everyone* has Facebook. *(An untrue statement. So unless one is sure that EVERYONE or EVERYBODY is involved, then it is safe to use them.)*
I, You, We, Us and Our	Do not use these pronouns unless your opinion is required i.e. What do you think / what is your view / opinion of ...? **If you read articles in the paper and magazines and listen and watch the news on radio and television, these pronouns are rarely used except in quotes.**
At there & at here	These are direct translations from Chinese but in English, the *at* is omitted. Note the example given.

	• Place the book there. ✓
	• Place the book at there. ✗
Do, go, take, & make	These verbs are general in description and do not do justice when describing specific actions. Note the following examples given.
	Example 1:
	• She **goes to serve** the customers. (**goes** is not necessary. Remember the general rule of using only one subject and one verb in a sentence).
	• She **serves** customers. (This is a better alternative)
	Example 2:
	• **Question:** What does your father do? **Answer:** He is in construction. He **makes** buildings. (The better verb would be **builds** or **constructs**).
	Example 3:
	• You should not **do** it like that. **Do** it like this! (This is acceptable in a conversation but not in writing essays.)
Ask & call	**Ask** and **call** are often misunderstood as **tell**. Note the examples given.
	Example 1:
	• Didn't I **ask** you to turn to page 32?! ✗ Didn't I **tell** you to turn to page 32?! ✓
	Example 2:
	• I **called** you to come to the front! ✗ I **told** you to come to the front! ✓
let	Let means to permit. In Chinese and Malay, objects are expressed in a way that they could permit someone to do something but which is incomprehensible in English. Note the example given.
	• The internet can **let** us know a lot of

	information. ✗ • The internet **provides** information. ✓
Between ... to	This is a common mistake. • Between ... and ... ✓ • From ... to ... ✓ • Between ... to ... ✗ • From ... and ... ✗
And so on	This phrase is informal. Replace the phrase with *etc.*
A, An and The	**A** and **An** are often left out. They should always be written before one countable subject or noun. **The** is often used by many in every sentence even when not required. **The** should only be used in two situations. • To refer to the only one that exists i.e. the sun, the prime minister of Japan, etc. • To refer to something that is already known. For example, there is a book on the table. **The** book belongs to him.
Its or It's	**Its** means something belonging to a thing or an object. **It's** is the short form of **it is**.
of	**Of** if used too often is considered old English. Note the example given. • The president of Junior Chamber International **of** Bangkok. ✗ • The Bangkok Junior Chamber International president. ✓ **Of** is often not necessary. Not the example given. • The town of Lahad Datu ✗ • Lahad Datu Town ✓

EDITING 1 PRACTICE

The following passage needs editing. Edit them accordingly. Remember to check that each sentence is structured correctly, the right tense is used and words and phrases to be avoided are excluded.

Many company in Malaysia can offers job vacancy from the general clerk to plantation managers. Unfortunately, everyone often are reject due to their monolingual proficiency.

Not acceptable are broken language at work. With many company investing overseas and merging with foreign company, knowing only one language put one at the end of the employment queue. While is important science and mathematics, communication in general not expressed in formulas and number.

They say charity begin at home and education does so. Many peoples forget that in many case, success is comes through hardship. It is not uncommon for parents especially in South East Asia to supporting their young adult childs. And common it is also that many parent are withdraw their kid from academic courses when they is seeming tough.

Thus, this can give rise to monolingual society because when learning one or two more languages seem impossible, abandonments follow. When learning is becoming impossible, there have no hope for the future. Some opinion may differ but this fact is remains, unless person is medically classified mentally challenged, stupidity not exist in this world. On the other hand, laziness are nurturing from young.

CORRECTION

Plenty of vacancies but few qualified applicants

EDITING 2

The following passage needs editing. Edit them accordingly. Remember to check that each sentence is structured correctly, the right tense is used, and words and phrases to be avoided are excluded.

Set up in 1989, Alice's restaurant is famous for it's tasty steamed buns, soupy dim sums, traditional cakes, Hainanese chicken rices and spicy tom yam. Its a family business run by a Muslim couples, so 'halal' foods are guaranteed.

There have two key word given priority at Alice's: Quality and Cleanliness. They very much part of Alice's formula to long running business.

Located in the heart of Kim Fung town, the ambience at Alice's are remaining the same except for a few wall decoration and the grade A certificates awarded by the Ministry of Health. Many regular is feeling very much at home at Alice's.

Alice, the manager, learnt the art of culinary from foreign chef and bakers, and also from those whose creation were coming straight from their home kitchens. Having at least two decade of cooking experiences in culinary science and the sheer love for cooking, Alice is a master of modification and until today, her modified recipes remains a secret.

Already in their 70s, Alice and Mahsan still runs their business with the assistance of their childs. They are friendly and are accustomed to with customers having a good chat.

CORRECTION

The First Chinese Muslim restaurant in town

EDITING 3

The following passage needs editing. Edit them accordingly. Remember to check that each sentence is structured correctly, the right tenses are used, and words and phrases to be avoided are excluded.

In 2010, I sign on the dotted line and join the Toastmasters Club. It take me 2 year to conjure up the courage to put myself in the spotlight and speaking in public. I experiences everything a virgin public speaker would usually go through. I has sweaty palm, palpitations, butterflies, etc. Fortunately, not did I wetted my pants.

Speaking in public is no doubt a harrowing ordeal but once the skills is mastered and the fidgeting controlled, the door of opportunity open naturally. Public speaking an important part of communication which not only expand a person's social and professional networks, but it also will lead to a better career and life quality.

Toastmasters' meetings never short of laughter too. People gets kicks out of presenting humorous speeches and the people gets to relax and enjoying their evenings with some wholesome entertainment. In addition, Toastmasters are put fun in learning. Members are allowed to make mistake and the more presentation maked, the more a person will improve particularly in body language and vocal variety.

I never regretted my decision to join the club. My speaking skills is more refined and my confidence is superb. Put me in front of a thousand peoples and I guarantees that my palms remains dry, the butterflies and palpitations ceases to exists and my pants is zipped, and ready I am for action.

CORRECTION

A Toastmaster's Address

_____

_____

_____

_____

_____

_____

_____

_____

_____

_____

_____

_____

_____

_____

_____

_____

_____

_____

_____

_____

_____

_____

CHAPTER 2

ESSAY WRITING
UNDERSTANDING QUESTIONS & TOPICS

Fewer Mistakes, Greater Confidence!

Most essay topics are made up of 3 components: **Content (Subject Matter),
Limiting Word(s) and D-Words.**

CONTENT

Content is a topic or a thing which can be studied. Note the examples given.

- Explain the differences between *studying* overseas and at home.

    '*studying*' is the content.

- Describe the common types of *food* in your country.

    '*food*' is the content.

Must remember!

The content guides writers from going out of topic. If a description of beverages is
included in the second topic 'food', then the description fails to fulfill the topic
requirement.

PRACTICE

Identify and underline the Content word(s)

1. Define 'beauty' and describe how beauty is perceived today.

2. The advantages and disadvantages of freedom of speech.

3. 'Money is not everything.' Do you agree?

4. Is killing ever justified?

5. 'Being an entertainer is not all glitzy.' What do you think?

6. Why is it difficult to learn a new language?

7. What is your view of military service being made obligatory?

8. To what extent is home schooling effective?

9. Describe the activities of religious people in your country.

10. Discuss the case for and against gay marriages.

THE LIMITING WORD(S)

The limiting word(s) restricts the coverage of a topic. Note the example given.

- Explain the differences between studying *overseas* and *at home*.
  '*overseas...at home*' are the limiting words.

- Illustrate the common types of food *in your country*.
  '*in your country*' are the limiting words.

PRACTICE

Identify and underline the Limiting word(s)

1. Is population control necessary in China?

2. How popular is KPOP in your country?

3. Discuss the advantages and disadvantages of YouTube.

4. Consider the practical measures in controlling an outbreak such as H7N9.

5. Should politics be taught in secondary or high school?

6. Children are sometimes demanding. To what extent should parents follow their demands?

7. Do entrepreneurs go for status upgrade or financial promotions?

8. Is it practical to have singing and dancing as part of co-curricular activities?

9. What is your view of an honest business person?

10. Do you think it is possible to live without the internet today?

D-WORD(S)

D—Word(s) specifies the written approach. Each D-word has its own function. To understand the differences, look up the dictionary and find the definitions for the following D-Words:

Account for:

_____

_____

Analyse:

_____

_____

Compare:

_____

_____

Consider:

_____

_____

Define:

_____

_____

Describe:

_____

_____

Discuss:

_____

_____

Enumerate:

_____

_____

Evaluate:

_____

_____

Examine:

_____

_____

Explain:

_____

_____

Illustrate:

_____

_____

Outline:

_____

_____

Must remember!

Understanding the requirements of questions and topics prevents you from going out of topic. If you make grammatical mistakes, you are still granted marks but if you go out of topic, expect zero marks.

CHAPTER 3

ESSAY WRITING
HOW MANY WORDS?
Fewer Mistakes, Greater Confidence!

The most daunting task for many is to reach the total number of words required for an assignment. However, given the correct formula, writing a 250-word essay would be as short as 30 minutes or less. Writing an essay becomes less daunting when the total number of words is divided according to the percentage required in each essay component: **Introduction, Body and Conclusion.**

INTRODUCTION

The total number of words written in an introduction is generally 10% of the total essay length.

The following is an approximate total number of words required for a variety of essay lengths.

Length of essay	10% of total length
250 word	25 words
350 word	35 words
500 word	50 words
1000 word	100 words

BODY

The total number of words written is generally 70% of the total essay length.

The following is an approximate total number of words required for a variety of essay lengths.

Length of essay	70% of total length
250 word	175 words
350 word	245 words
500 word	350 words
1000 word	700 words

CONCLUSION

The total number of words written is generally 20% of the total essay length.

The following is an approximate total number of words required for a variety of essay lengths.

Length of essay	20% of total essay length
250 word	50 words
350 word	70 words
500 word	100 words
1000 word	200 words

Must remember!

The conventional method of writing an essay is to start with the introduction and end with the conclusion, but this may not be advisable for good reasons. The reasons are explained in the following chapters.

When writing an essay especially in an exam, it is better to write the body first, the introduction second and the conclusion last.

CHAPTER 4

ESSAY WRITING
THE BODY
FORMULA

Fewer Mistakes, Greater Confidence!

The body actually dictates the introduction and conclusion. So the body should always be written first. Furthermore, many fret about the body because it has the most number of words written compared to the introduction and the conclusion. So it is logical to tackle the most challenging component first.

Now that you know the total number of words required in the body of an essay regardless of its total word length, the next step is to divide the total number of words in the body with the number of paragraphs in it.

The following is a general guideline to the number of paragraphs required according to different essay lengths.

Length of essay	Minimum & Maximum number of paragraphs in the body	Total words according to the number of paragraphs
250 word	2 & 3	88 & 58 words
350 word	3 & 4	82 & 62 words
500 word	4 & 5	88 & 70 words
1000 word	5 & 6	140 & 117 words

Words of Comfort!

Writing 250 words may cause panic but writing between 58 and 140 words should not be a problem.

THE MAIN IDEA (TOPIC SENTENCE)   NOTES

Each paragraph in the body is divided into two sections: **The Main Idea** and **The Elaboration**.

FORMULA: Body

Main Idea + Elaboration

The main idea takes up 20% of the total number of words in a paragraph in the body. The following is a general guideline to the total words required for a main idea according to various essay lengths.

Length of essay	Approximate number of words required in writing a main idea
250 word	12 to 18 words
350 word	12 to 16 words
500 word	14 to 18 words
1000 word	23 to 28 words (about 2 to 3 sentences)

Must remember!

Writing below 12 words per sentence is not recommended for an essay with an essay length above 300 words. The total number of words per sentence should often be kept between 12 and 18 words for beginners and intermediate level.

UNDERSTANDING THE MAIN IDEA

Ask any teacher the meaning of a main idea and the most popular answer is **the most important idea of a topic.** That explanation may be easily understood by the general academic experts but to an average student, the explanation equals no explanation at all.

DEFINITION

The main idea is actually the direct answer to a question or a clear clarification of a topic written in a complete sentence or sentences.

Let's examine the following topic for a 250-word essay:

Reasons for students' academic failure
(Why do students fail in college?)

Must remember!

Many are taught to write ideas in point forms and then write them in complete sentences. To save time, go straight to writing the main ideas in complete sentences.

Must remember!

The main idea is the direct answer to the question or clarification of the topic in a complete sentence or sentences, and the total number of word range for the sentence is between 12 and 18.

Paragraph 1:

Main idea: (Why do students fail in school?) Start the answer after 'because'.

First answer / reason (main idea)

Many school graduates go for further studies without clear goals and effective study skills. (14 words)

Second answer or reason (main idea)

The majority who fail lack maturity and therefore are usually not disciplined. (12 words)

PRACTICE

Now, practise writing the main ideas for the following questions and topics.

How does technology affect the way daily activities are done?

First answer: State the way technology affects one or two daily activities.

_____

_____

(words)

Second answer: State the way technology affects other daily activities.

_____

_____

(words)

Discuss the case for and against trading online.

First answer: State the case for trading online.

_____

_____

(words)

Second answer: State the case against trading online.

_____

_____

(words)

Time or Money?

First answer: Compare and state the importance of one subject over the other.

_____

_____

(words)

Second answer: State another importance of one subject over the other.

_____

_____

(words)

ELABORATION

Now that you have a clearer picture of how to write the main ideas or topic sentences, let's proceed to writing the elaboration.

DEFINITION

Elaboration is a detailed explanation of the main idea with or without examples and whenever possible, without repeating the words in the main idea. Examine the following examples.

EXAMPLE 1:

Alan's sister is beautiful. She has an oval shaped face with big blue eyes and natural pink pouty lips. Her skin is fair and flawless, and her hair is silky smooth. She is tall and slim. She is comparable to the German supermodel Claudia Schiffer.

THE BREAK DOWN

Main idea:	Alan's sister is beautiful.
Elaboration:	She has an oval shaped face with big blue eyes and natural pink pouty lips. Her skin is fair and flawless, and her hair is silky smooth. She is tall and slim.
Example:	She is comparable to the German supermodel Claudia Schiffer.

EXAMPLE 2:

Facebook is free, and it is opened to anyone with internet access. There are no membership and entrance fees needed to join this utility. Needless to say, similar to free emails, it attracts millions of users. There are also no admission limitations based on class, gender and profession that prevent admittance. However, there is an age limit but many are able to bluff their way to opening an account.

THE BREAK DOWN

Main idea 1:   Facebook is free

Elaboration 1:   There is no membership and entrance fee needed to join this utility. Needless to say, it attracts millions of users.

Example: similar to free emails

Main idea 2:   It is opened to anyone with internet access.

Elaboration 1:   There are also no admission limitations based on class, gender and profession that prevent acceptance. However, there is an age limit but many are able to bluff their way to opening an account.

Example: *None*

Thus, the elaborations to the previous essay topic are written as follows:

Reasons for students' academic failure
(Why do students fail in college?)

Paragraph 1:

Many school graduates go for further studies without clear goals and effective study skills. Generally, students of such level are clueless of the steps required to succeed academically. They understand that they have to study and sit for exams but they are ignorant of the requirements. Thus, without any obvious direction, failure is a great possibility. Having poor study skills is also a major factor which contributes to educational disappointments. The necessary study skills include time management, note taking techniques, getting the right information, etc.

THE BREAK DOWN

Main idea 1:	**Many high or secondary school graduates go for further studies without clear goals.**
Elaboration 1:	Generally, students of such level are clueless of the steps required to succeed academically. They understand that they have to study and sit for exams but they are ignorant of the requirements. Thus, without any obvious direction, failure is a great possibility.
Example:	None
Main idea 2:	**Many school graduates go for further studies without effective study skills.**
Elaboration 2:	Having poor study skills is also a major factor which contributes to educational disappointments.
Example:	The necessary study skills include time management, note taking techniques, getting the right information, etc.

Paragraph 2:

The majority who fail lack maturity and therefore are usually not disciplined. Some perceive that college is a means of meeting new friends and having a good time. At such an age, youths are likely to enjoy themselves first than think of their priorities. Most of them have problems keeping up with assignments. Naturally, self-discipline is a problem. College students are vulnerable to peer pressure and have difficulties in rejecting temptations such as invitations to social gatherings and pointless and unnecessary entertainment.

THE BREAK DOWN

Main idea 1:	**The majority who fail lack maturity**
Elaboration 1:	Some perceive that going for further studies is a means of meeting new friends, partying and having a good time. At such an age, youths are likely to enjoy themselves first than think of their priorities. Most of them have problems keeping up with assignments.
Example:	None

Main idea 2:	**Therefore, the majority is usually not disciplined.**
Elaboration 2:	College students are vulnerable to peer pressure and have difficulties in rejecting temptations.
Example:	such as invitations to social gatherings and pointless and unnecessary entertainment.

Must remember!

Good elaborations often do not include the words used in the main ideas. If you reread the previous two paragraphs, words in the main ideas are not repeated in the elaborations.

If the total number of words in a paragraph is minimal, then it is recommended that only one elaboration is needed but if you are required to write more or a longer paragraph, then you may opt to write two elaborations as exemplified. Again, it is advisable to write the elaboration in complete sentences to save time. Writing short notes and then referring back to them just to transform them into complete sentences waste time.

PRACTICE

Now, practise writing the elaborations for the main ideas of the previous essay questions and topics.

How does technology affect the way daily activities are done?

Rewrite the first main idea for reference. Copy it from the previous practice.

_____

_____

Write the elaboration in about 70 words.

_____

_____

_____

_____

_____

_____

_____

_____

_____

_____

Rewrite the second main idea for reference. Copy it from the previous practice.

_____

_____

Write the elaboration.

_____

_____

EDITING CHECKLIST

Place ✓ in the following boxes to ensure that the writing style and content follow the instructions and formulas.

- ❑ Each sentence is correctly structured.
- ❑ The appropriate tense is used consistently.
- ❑ *Words and phrases to avoid* are excluded.
- ❑ Words other than the content and limiting words in the main ideas are not repeated in the elaborations.
- ❑ The elaborations explain the main ideas in detail.
- ❑ The total number of words is within the recommended word total.

Discuss the case for and against trading online.

Rewrite the first main idea for reference. Copy it from the previous practice.

Write the elaboration in about 70 words.

Rewrite the second main idea for reference. Copy it from the previous practice.

Write the elaboration.

EDITING CHECKLIST

Place ✓ in the following boxes to ensure that the writing style and content follow the instructions and formulas.

- ❑   Each sentence is correctly structured.
- ❑   The appropriate tense is used consistently.
- ❑   **Words and phrases to avoid** are excluded.
- ❑   Words other than the content and limiting words in the main ideas are not repeated in the elaborations.
- ❑   The elaborations explain the main ideas in detail.
- ❑   The total number of words is within the recommended word total.

Time or Money?

Rewrite the first main idea for reference. Copy it from the previous practice.

_____

_____

Write the elaboration in about 70 words.

_____

_____

_____

_____

_____

_____

_____

_____

_____

_____

_____

Rewrite the second main idea for reference. Copy it from the previous practice.

_____

_____

Write the elaboration.

_____

_____

_____

_____

_____

_____

EDITING CHECKLIST

Place ✓ in the following boxes to ensure that the writing style and content follow the instructions and formulas.

❑ Each sentence is correctly structured.

❑ The appropriate tense is used consistently.

❑ ***Words and phrases to avoid*** are excluded.

❑ Words other than the content and limiting words in the main ideas are not repeated in the elaborations.

❑ The elaborations explain the main ideas in detail.

❑ The total number of words is within the recommended word total.

SUMMARY OF THE BODY FORMULA

FORMULAS

- **Total number of words required in the body**
  70-% x Essay length

- **Total number of words required in the main idea**
  20% x total number of words in a paragraph

- **Main Idea or Topic Sentence**
  20% X total number of words in a paragraph

- **Elaboration**
  80% x total number of words in a paragraph

- **Body**
  Main Ideas + Elaborations

DEFINITIONS

- **Main Idea**
  The main idea is actually the direct answer to a question or a clear clarification of a topic written in a complete sentence or sentences.
  (*Note: It is possible to write two or more ideas in a sentence*).

- **Elaboration**
  A detailed explanation of the main idea or ideas with or without examples.

PRACTICE

TIMED TEST

Now that you understand the formula to writing the body, learn to write the body of a 250-word essay in 30 minutes. However, this is easier said than done because many panic under pressure, and old habits die hard. Giving up old habits and learning new ones often take three attempts. So try these three tests and time yourself. Honesty pays off.

FIRST ATTEMPT

Write the body to the following question in about 175 words.

Start Time: _____   End Time: _____

Should children with special needs be prevented from going to school?

_____

_____

_____

_____

_____

_____

_____

_____

_____

_____

_____

_____

_____

_____

_____

--(words)

EDITING CHECKLIST

Place ✓ in the following boxes to ensure that the writing style and content follow the instructions and formulas.

- ❑   Each sentence is structured correctly.
- ❑   The appropriate tense is used consistently.
- ❑   ***Words and phrases to avoid*** are excluded.
- ❑   Words other than the content and limiting words in the main ideas are not repeated in the elaboration.
- ❑   The elaborations explain the main ideas in detail.
- ❑   The total number of words is within the recommended word total.

SECOND ATTEMPT

Write the body to the following question in about 175 words.

Start Time: _____   End Time: _____

To what extent should tradition be followed?

_____

_____

_____

_____

_____

_____

_____

_____

_____

_____

_____

_____

_____

_____

_____

_____

_____

_____

_____

_____

- -

- -

- -

- -

- -

- -

- -

- -

- -

- -

- -

- -

- -

- -

_____ (words)

EDITING CHECKLIST

Place ✓ in the following boxes to ensure that the writing style and content follow the instructions and formulas.

- ❏ Each sentence is structured correctly.
- ❏ The appropriate tense is used consistently.
- ❏ **Words and phrases to avoid** are excluded.
- ❏ Words other than the content and limiting words in the main ideas are not repeated in the elaboration.
- ❏ The elaborations explain the main ideas in detail.
- ❏ The total number of words is within the recommended word total.

THIRD ATTEMPT

Write the body to the following question in about 175 words.

Start Time: _____   End Time: _____

Advanced technology has its downside. Describe life without technology?

_____ (words)

EDITING CHECKLIST

Place ✓ in the following boxes to ensure that the writing style and content follow the instructions and formulas.

- ❑ Each sentence is structured correctly.
- ❑ The appropriate tense is used consistently.
- ❑ ***Words and phrases to avoid*** are excluded.
- ❑ Words other than the content and limiting words in the main ideas are not repeated in the elaboration.
- ❑ The elaborations explain the main ideas in detail.
- ❑ The total number of words is within the recommended word total.

CHAPTER 5

ESSAY WRITING
THE INTRODUCTION FORMULA

Fewer Mistakes, Greater Confidence!

The introduction is the easiest component to write. It follows a standard guideline which includes the main ideas written in the body.

FORMULA: Introduction

General Statement + General Answer to Question + The list of main ideas

General Statement

Write a general statement on the subject or main topic of the question: **Reasons for students' academic failure**. The main topic in this question is *students*. Tap into your own experience and knowledge of students going for tertiary studies. It can be written in any way you deem fit.

Option 1:

Every year, many students go straight to college after graduating from high school.

Option 2:

Students who plan to get better jobs often study until they get at least a degree.

Option 3:

College is usually the next destination for students who complete their high school studies.

General Answer To The Question

The second sentence addresses the question in general often without giving the specifics or details.

Option 1:

Students' academic failure is due to several reasons.

Option 2:

There are a few reasons for students' academic failure.

Option 3:

However, many fail in college.

The List Of Main Ideas

List the main ideas as written in the body. Thus, it is necessary to write the body first before the introduction and conclusion.

Option 1:

The reasons include having no clear goals and effective study, and the lack of maturity and discipline.

Option 2:

The main reasons for their failure are many do not have clear goals, effective study skills, maturity and discipline.

Option 3:

In addition to not having clear goals and effective study skills, they lack maturity and discipline.

THE FINAL DRAFT OF THE INTRODUCTION

Reasons for students' academic failure
(Why do students fail in college?)

College is usually the next destination for students who complete high school. However, many fail and their academic failure is due to several reasons. The reasons include having no clear goals and effective study skills, and the lack of maturity and discipline.

PRACTICE

Now, practise writing the introduction for the previous essay questions and topics.

How does technology affect the way daily activities are done?

General statement:

_____

_____

General answer to the question:

_____

_____

List the main ideas in a complete sentence:

_____

_____

Discuss the case for and against trading online?

General statement:

_____

_____

General answer to the question:

_____

_____

List the main ideas in a complete sentence:

_____

_____

Time or Money?

General statement:

_____

_____

General answer to the question:

_____

_____

List the main ideas in a complete sentence:

_____

_____

EDITING CHECKLIST

Place ✓ in the following boxes to ensure that the introduction follows the instructions and formula.

❑　　Each sentence is structured correctly.

❑　　The appropriate tense is used consistently.

❑　　The first sentence is a general statement of the content.

❑　　The second sentence is the general answer to the question.

❑　　The total number of words is within the recommended word total.

SUMMARY OF INTRODUCTION FORMULA

FORMULAS

- **Total number of words required in the introduction**
  10% x Essay length

- **Introduction**
  General Statement + General Answer to Question + The List Of Main Ideas

DEFINITION

- **General Statement**
  Any information pertaining to the content.

CHAPTER 6

ESSAY WRITING
THE CONCLUSION FORMULA

Fewer Mistakes, Greater Confidence!

The conclusion is a summary of the body. Often, the paragraphs are shortened and rephrased.

FORMULA: Conclusion

General Answer to Question + Summary of the body

The first line of the conclusion is the general answer to the question similar to the second sentence in the introduction.

Reasons for students' academic failure
(Why do students fail in college?)

First line:

Start the sentence with one of the following concluding phrases followed by the general answer to the essay question.

In conclusion / In a nutshell / To summarise / In short,
students fail for two main reasons:

- They have no clear goals and effective study skills, and

- Many lack maturity and self-discipline.

Must remember!

There are many ways to rephrase the main ideas or topic sentences. There is no right way to rephrasing a sentence but precise meaning and correct grammar are important. Note the following examples.

1. **Students have no clear goals and effective study skills.**

Example 1:

Many fail because they lack clear visions and proper study skills.

Example 2:

Without distinct objectives and effective learning methods, many students fail.

Example 3:

Students' academic failure is due to unclear purposes and good study habits.

2. **Many lack maturity and self-discipline.**

Example 1:

Many are immature and reckless.

Example 2:

The absence of wisdom and self-control bring about students' academic failure.

Example 3:

Students are immature and vulnerable to their environment.

Ideally, the first line of the conclusion should be between 10 and 15 words for a 250-word essay but not always. The final draft of the first line is written as follows:

In conclusion, many college students fail as they have no distinct objectives and learning methods, and are lacking in wisdom and self-control.

PRACTICE

Now, practise writing the first line of the conclusion for the three questions given previously. Write 2 rephrased sentences for practice. You should refer to the main ideas written in the previous practices.

How does technology affect the way daily activities are done?

Rewrite main idea 1 here for easy reference. Copy it from the previous practice.

Rephrased Idea 1:

Rephrased Idea 2:

Rewrite main idea 2 here for easy reference. Copy it from the previous practice.

Rephrased Idea 1:

Rephrased Idea 2:

Discuss the case for and against trading online.

Rewrite main idea 1 here for easy reference. Copy it from the previous practice.

_____
_____

Rephrased Idea 1:

_____
_____

Rephrased Idea 2:

_____
_____

Rewrite main idea 2 here for easy reference. Copy it from the previous practice.

_____
_____

Rephrased Idea 1:

_____
_____

Rephrased Idea 2:

_____
_____

Time or Money?

Rewrite main idea 1 here for easy reference. Copy it from the previous practice.

Rephrased Idea 1:

Rephrased Idea 2:

Rewrite main idea 2 here for easy reference. Copy it from the previous practice.

Rephrased Idea 1:

Rephrased Idea 2:

The balance of the conclusion is left for the summary of the elaboration of each paragraph in the body. For example, if the total number of words in the conclusion is 50 and the total number of words in the first sentence of the conclusion is 10, then the balance is 40 words.

SUMMARY OF THE ELABORATION

Again, there are no right ways of starting and rephrasing a sentence as long as the meaning is the same. As a general rule, summarising requires the exclusion of the following:

- Examples,
- Repetitive and Descriptive words,
- Phrases which express the same or similar meaning, and
- Lengthy expressions.

FORMULA: Summary

The Body – (Examples + Repetitive Words + Descriptive Words + Phrases with the same or similar meanings + Lengthy Expressions) + Conjunctions and/or Connecting Words

Examine the following exclusions:

Reasons for students' academic failure
(Why do students fail in college?)

The elaboration for paragraph 1 in the body:

Generally, students ~~of such level~~ are clueless of the steps required to succeed ~~academically. They understand that they have to study and sit for exams but they are ignorant of the requirements.~~ Thus, without any obvious direction, failure is a great possibility. Having poor study skills is also a ~~major~~ factor ~~which contributes to educational disappointments. The necessary study skills include time management, note taking techniques, getting the right information, etc.~~

So, the remaining text is written as follows:

Generally, students are clueless of the steps required to succeed. Thus, without any obvious direction, failure is a great possibility. Having poor study skills is also a factor.

To further shorten the summary, replace long phrases with a word or two. Compare the following paragraphs.

- **Generally, students** are clueless of the steps required to succeed. Thus, without any obvious direction, failure is **a great possibility**. Having poor study skills is also a factor. (28 words)

- **Many** are clueless of the steps to succeed. Thus, without any obvious directions, failure is **probable**. Having poor study skills is also a factor. (24 words)

Another method is to combine sentences with conjunctions or connecting words. Examine the example given. Compare the following paragraphs.

- Many are clueless of the steps to succeed. **Thus, without any obvious directions, failure is probable. Having poor study skills is also a factor.** (24 words)

- Many are clueless of the steps to succeed. **Thus, without any obvious directions and proper study skills,** failure is probable. (20 words)

Examine the following process of summarizing the elaboration of paragraph 2 in the body.

~~At such an age~~, youths are likely to enjoy themselves first than think of their priorities. ~~Most of them have problems keeping up with assignments.~~ Naturally, self-discipline is a problem. College students are vulnerable to peer pressure and have difficulties in rejecting temptations ~~such as invitations to social gatherings and pointless and unnecessary entertainment.~~

So, the remaining text is written as follows:

Youths are likely to enjoy themselves first than think of their priorities. Naturally, self-discipline is a problem. College students are vulnerable to peer pressure and have difficulties in rejecting temptations. (30 words)

To further shorten the summary, replace long phrases with a word or two. Compare the following paragraphs:

- Youths **are likely to** enjoy themselves first than think of their priorities. Naturally, self-discipline is a problem. College students are vulnerable to peer pressure **and have difficulties in rejecting** temptations. (30 words)

- Youths **like to** enjoy themselves first than think of their priorities. Naturally, self-discipline is a problem. **Most are vulnerable to peer pressure and temptations**. (24 words)

Another method is to combine sentences with conjunctions or connecting words. Examine the example given. Compare the following paragraphs.

- **Youths like to enjoy themselves first than think of their priorities. Naturally, self-discipline is a problem.** Most are vulnerable to peer pressure and temptations. (24 words)

- **Youths are generally not self-disciplined and often think of enjoying themselves first.** Most are vulnerable to peer pressure and temptations. (20 words)

So the final draft of the conclusion is written as follows:

THE FINAL DRAFT OF THE CONCLUSION
(Combine the first line and the rephrased sentences)

Reasons for students' academic failure
(Why do students fail in college?)

In conclusion, many college students fail as they have no distinct objectives and learning methods, and are lacking in wisdom and self-control. Many are clueless of the steps to succeed. Furthermore, they are generally not self-disciplined and often think of enjoying themselves first. Most are vulnerable to peer pressure and temptations.

Now practise writing your own summary.

How does technology affect the way daily activities are done?

For easy reference, copy the elaboration in paragraph 1 of the body previously written.

_____

_____

_____

_____

_____

_____

_____

_____

Cross out the examples, repetitive and descriptive words, phrases which express the same or similar meanings and lengthy expressions.

Write the remaining text below.

_____

_____

_____

To further shorten the summary, replace long phrases with a word or two.

_____

_____

_____

Combine sentences where possible.

_____

_____

_____

For easy reference, copy the elaboration in paragraph 2 of the body previously written.

_____

_____

_____

_____

_____

_____

_____

_____

_____

_____

_____

Cross out the examples, repetitive and descriptive words, phrases which express the same or similar meanings and lengthy expressions.

Write the remaining text below.

_____

_____

_____

To further shorten the summary, replace long phrases with a word or two.

_____

_____

_____

Combine sentences where possible.

_____

_____

_____

THE FINAL DRAFT OF THE CONCLUSION
(Combine the first line and the summary)
How does technology affect the way daily activities are done?

EDITING CHECKLIST

Place ✓ in each the following boxes to ensure that the conclusion follows the instructions and formula.

❑   Each sentence is structured correctly.

❑   The appropriate tense is used consistently.

❑   The first sentence re-answers the question in general.

❑   The summary excludes examples, repetitive and descriptive words, phrases with the same or similar meanings and lengthy expressions.

❑   The total number of words is within the recommended word total.

Discuss the case for and against trading online.

For easy reference, copy the elaboration in paragraph 1 of the body previously written.

Cross out the examples, repetitive and descriptive words, phrases which express the same or similar meanings and lengthy expressions.

Write the remaining text below.

To further shorten the summary, replace long phrases with a word or two.

Combine sentences where possible.

For easy reference, copy the elaboration in paragraph 2 of the body previously written.

_____

_____

_____

_____

_____

_____

_____

_____

_____

_____

_____

Cross out the examples, repetitive and descriptive words, phrases which express the same or similar meanings and lengthy expressions.

Write the remaining text below.

_____

_____

_____

To further shorten the summary, replace long phrases with a word or two.

_____

_____

_____

Combine sentences where possible.

_____

_____

_____

THE FINAL DRAFT OF THE CONCLUSION
(Combine the first line and the summary)
Discuss the case for and against trading online.

EDITING CHECKLIST

Place ✓ in each the following boxes to ensure that the conclusion follows the instructions and formula.

❑   Each sentence is structured correctly.

❑   The appropriate tense is used consistently.

❑   The first sentence re-answers the question in general.

❑   The summary excludes examples, repetitive and descriptive words, phrases with the same or similar meanings and lengthy expressions.

❑   The total number of words is within the recommended word total.

Time or Money?

For easy reference, copy the elaboration in paragraph 1 of the body previously written.

_____

_____

_____

_____

_____

_____

_____

_____

_____

_____

Cross out the examples, repetitive and descriptive words, phrases which express the same or similar meanings and lengthy expressions.

Write the remaining text below.

_____

_____

_____

To further shorten the summary, replace long phrases with a word or two.

_____

_____

_____

Combine sentences where possible.

_____

_____

_____

For easy reference, copy the elaboration in paragraph 2 of the body previously written.

Cross out the examples, repetitive and descriptive words, and phrases which express the same or similar meanings and lengthy expressions.

Write the remaining text below.

To further shorten the summary, replace long phrases with a word or two.

Combine sentences where possible.

THE FINAL DRAFT OF THE CONCLUSION
(Combine the first line and the summary)
Time or Money?

_____

_____

_____

_____

_____

_____

_____

_____

_____

EDITING CHECKLIST

Place ✓ in each the following boxes to ensure that the conclusion follows the instructions and formula.

- ❑ Each sentence is structured correctly.
- ❑ The appropriate tense is used consistently.
- ❑ The first sentence re-answers the question in general.
- ❑ The summary excludes examples, repetitive and descriptive words, phrases with the same or similar meanings and lengthy expressions.
- ❑ The total number of words is within the recommended word total.

SUMMARY OF CONCLUSION FORMULA

FORMULAS

- **Total number of words required in the conclusion**
  20% x Essay length

- **Conclusion**
  Concluding Phrase + General Answer to the question + Summary of body

- **Summary**
  The Body – (Examples + Repetitive Words + Descriptive Words + Phrases with the same or similar meanings + Lengthy Expressions) + Conjunctions and/or Connecting words

THE COMPLETE ESSAY
Reasons for students' academic failure
(Why students fail in college?)

College is usually the next destination for students who complete high school. However, many fail and their academic failure is due to several reasons. The reasons include having no clear goals and effective study skills, and the lack of maturity and discipline.

Many school graduates go for further studies without clear goals and effective study skills. Generally, students of such level are clueless of the steps required to succeed academically. They understand that they have to study and sit for exams, but they are ignorant of the requirements. Thus, without any obvious direction, failure is a great possibility. Having poor study skills is also a major factor which contributes to educational disappointments. The necessary study skills include time management, note taking techniques, getting the right information, etc.

The majority who fail lack maturity and therefore are usually not disciplined. Some perceive that college is a means of meeting new friends and having a good time. At such an age, youths are likely to enjoy themselves first than think of their priorities. Most of them have problems keeping up with assignments. Naturally, self-discipline is a problem. College students are vulnerable to peer pressure and have difficulties in rejecting temptations such as invitations to social gatherings and pointless and unnecessary entertainment.

In conclusion, many college students fail as they have no distinct academic objectives and effective learning methods, and are lacking in wisdom and self-control. Many are clueless of the steps to succeed. Furthermore, they are generally not self-disciplined and often think of enjoying themselves first. Most are vulnerable to peer pressure and temptations.

(262 words)

YOUR COMPLETE ESSAY

Based on the previous question, copy the paragraphs in order.

How does technology affect the way daily activities are done?

_____

_____

_____

_____

_____

_____

_____

_____

_____

_____

_____

_____

_____

_____

_____

_____

_____

_____

_____

_____

_____

_____

_____

_____

_____

_____

_____

_____

_____

_____

_____

_____

_____

_____

_____

_____

_____

_____

_____

_____

_____

_____

_____

_____(words)

YOUR COMPLETE ESSAY

Based on the previous question, copy the paragraphs in order.

Discuss the case for and against trading online.

_____

_____

_____

_____

_____

_____

_____

_____

_____

_____

_____

_____

_____

_____

_____

_____

_____

_____

_____

_____

_____

_____

_____(words)

YOUR COMPLETE ESSAY

Based on the previous question, copy the paragraphs in order.

Time or Money?

_____
_____
_____
_____
_____
_____
_____
_____
_____
_____
_____
_____
_____
_____
_____
_____
_____
_____
_____
_____
_____
_____

_____

_____

_____

_____

_____

_____

_____

_____

_____

_____

_____

_____

_____

_____

_____

_____

_____

_____

_____

_____

_____

_____

_____

_____(words)

CHAPTER 7

ESSAY WRITING
PRACTICE MAKES PERFECT

Fewer Mistakes, Greater Confidence!

Practise writing an essay at least three times a month. The following essay practices are timed tests. The first three tests should be completed within 40 minutes and the next three should be completed within 30 minutes.

MUST REMEMBER!

To score in essays, you have to apply the tips and formulas learnt.

- The Fundamentals
- Understanding essay questions so you do not go out of topic
- Remember the total number of words
- Write the body first, starting with the main ideas followed by the elaborations
- Write the introduction second and according to its formula.
- Write the conclusion last and according to its formula. Make sure the total number of words in each component is within the word limit.
- Edit

The key is to minimize mistakes and maximize marks!

250-WORD ESSAY IN 40 MINUTES

Start Time: _____   End Time: _____

Do you believe that humans are generally self-centered?

_____

_____

_____

_____

_____

_____

_____

_____

_____

_____

_____

_____

_____

_____

_____

_____

_____

_____

_____

_____

_____

_____

_____

_____

_____ (words)

250-WORD ESSAY IN 40 MINUTES

Start Time: _____   End Time: _____

Explain the impact of natural disasters on the global economy.

_____

_____

_____

_____

_____

_____

_____

_____

_____

_____

_____

_____

_____

_____

_____

_____

_____

_____

_____

_____

_____

_____

_____

_____

_____

_____

_____

_____

_____

_____

_____

_____

_____

_____

_____

_____

_____

_____

_____

_____

_____

_____(words)

250-WORD ESSAY IN 40 MINUTES

Start Time: _____   End Time: _____

Discuss the future of recycled fashion.

_____

_____

_____

_____

_____

_____

_____

_____

_____

_____

_____

_____

_____

_____

_____

_____

_____

_____

_____

_____

_____
_____
_____
_____
_____
_____
_____
_____
_____
_____
_____
_____
_____
_____
_____
_____
_____
_____
_____
_____
_____
_____
_____
_____ (words)

250-WORD ESSAY IN 30 MINUTES

Start Time: _____   End Time: _____

Describe the function of a family in a community.

_____

_____

_____

_____

_____

_____

_____

_____

_____

_____

_____

_____

_____

_____

_____

_____

_____

_____

_____

_____

_____

_____

_____

_____ (words)

250-WORD ESSAY IN 30 MINUTES

Start Time: _____   End Time: _____

Define peace and its implications.

_____

_____

_____

_____

_____

_____

_____

_____

_____

_____

_____

_____

_____

_____

_____

_____

_____

_____

_____

_____

_____

_____

_____

_____

_____

_____

_____

_____

_____

_____

_____

_____

_____

_____

_____

_____

_____

_____

_____

_____

_____

_____

_____

_____(words)

250-WORD ESSAY IN 30 MINUTES

Start Time: _____   End Time: _____

In your view, what is the possibility of man conquering space?

_____

_____

_____

_____

_____

_____

_____

_____

_____

_____

_____

_____

_____

_____

_____

_____

_____

_____

_____

_____

_____

_____

_____

_____

_____

_____

_____

_____

_____

_____

_____

_____

_____

_____

_____

_____

_____

_____

_____

_____

_____

_____

_____

_____(words)

Now that you have practised writing 250-word essays, try writing 350-word essays. Remember to apply the tips and formulas learnt so that you complete the essays within the time given and with minimal mistakes.

350-WORD ESSAY IN 60 MINUTES

Start Time: _____   End Time: _____

Define effective communication.

_____

_____

_____

_____

_____

_____

_____

_____

_____

_____

_____

_____

_____

_____

_____

_____

_____

_____

_____

_____

_____

_____

_____

_____

_____ (words)

350-WORD ESSAY IN 60 MINUTES

Start Time: _____   End Time: _____

Why is it important to acquire good habits?

_____
_____
_____
_____
_____
_____
_____
_____
_____
_____
_____
_____
_____
_____
_____
_____
_____
_____
_____
_____
_____

_____
_____
_____
_____
_____
_____
_____
_____
_____
_____
_____
_____
_____
_____
_____
_____
_____
_____
_____
_____
_____
_____
_____
_____
_____(words)

350-WORD ESSAY IN 60 MINUTES

Start Time: _____   End Time: _____

Exemplify an ideal school or college.

_____

_____

_____

_____

_____

_____

_____

_____

_____

_____

_____

_____

_____

_____

_____

_____

_____

_____

_____

_____

_____

_____

_____

_____

_____ (words)

350-WORD ESSAY IN 45 MINUTES

Start Time: _____   End Time: _____

Discuss the pros and cons of a two-day weekend.

_____

_____

_____

_____

_____

_____

_____

_____

_____

_____

_____

_____

_____

_____

_____

_____

_____

_____

_____

_____

_____

_____

_____

_____

_____

_____

_____

_____

_____

_____

_____

_____

_____

_____

_____

_____

_____

_____

_____

_____

_____

_____

_____

_____(words)

350-WORD ESSAY IN 45 MINUTES

Start Time: _____   End Time: _____

Most, if not all, religions uphold good virtues. Why are there still those who do mischief?

_____
_____
_____
_____
_____
_____
_____
_____
_____
_____
_____
_____
_____
_____
_____
_____
_____
_____
_____
_____
_____
_____
_____
_____
_____
_____
_____(words)

350-WORD ESSAY IN 45 MINUTES

Start Time: _____   End Time: _____

Consider the influence of YouTube on globalization.

_____
_____
_____
_____
_____
_____
_____
_____
_____
_____
_____
_____
_____
_____
_____
_____
_____
_____
_____
_____
_____
_____

_____

_____

_____

_____

_____

_____

_____

_____

_____

_____

_____

_____

_____

_____

_____

_____

_____

_____

_____

_____

_____

_____

_____ (words)

Now that you are better at writing 250 to 350-word essays, practise writing 500-word essays. Writing a 500-word essay clearly requires more words and writing a sentence of more than 18 words is often difficult and confusing. Let's revise the total number of word division for a 500-word essay.

Introduction

10% of 500 words = 50 words (approximately)

Body

70% of 500 words = 350 words (approximately)

Conclusion

20% of 500 words = 100 words (approximately)

Must remember!

- In a 500-word essay, the suggested minimum number of paragraphs is 4 and the suggested maximum number of paragraphs is 5, so the total number of words per paragraph in the body is between 70 and 88 words. Thus, there is no cause for panic.

- However, the extension is in the introduction and conclusion. There is an increase of about 15 words in the introduction and an increase of about 30 words in the conclusion, which comes to about an addition of just one to two sentences.

- Basically, the general statement in the introduction can be lengthened and naturally the 30 words in the conclusion cover the extra paragraph in the body. So with that explained, proceed to writing 500-word essays.

500-WORD ESSAY IN 75 MINUTES

Start Time: _____   End Time: _____

Discuss the reliability of main stream media.

_____

_____

_____

_____

_____

_____

_____

_____

_____

_____

_____

_____

_____

_____

_____

_____

_____

_____

_____

_____

_____

_____

_____

_____

_____

_____

_____

_____

_____

_____

_____

_____

_____

_____

_____

_____

_____

_____

_____

_____

_____

_____

_____

_____ (words)

500-WORD ESSAY IN 75 MINUTES

Start Time: _____   End Time: _____

Consider methods to save money and suggest some investment possibilities.

_____

_____

_____

_____

_____

_____

_____

_____

_____

_____

_____

_____

_____

_____

_____

_____

_____

_____

_____

_____

_____

_____

_____

_____

_____

_____

_____

_____

_____

_____

_____

_____

_____

_____

_____

_____

_____

_____

_____

_____

_____

_____(words)

500-WORD ESSAY IN 75 MINUTES

Start Time: _____   End Time: _____

Explain the differences between an extrovert and an introvert.

_____

_____

_____

_____

_____

_____

_____

_____

_____

_____

_____

_____

_____

_____

_____

_____

_____

_____

_____

_____

_____

_____

_____

_____ (words)

500-WORD ESSAY IN 60 MINUTES

Start Time: _____   End Time: _____

Describe a known charity or non-government organisation.

_____

_____

_____

_____

_____

_____

_____

_____

_____

_____

_____

_____

_____

_____

_____

_____

_____

_____

_____

_____

_____

_____

_____

_____

_____

_____

_____

_____

_____

_____

_____

_____

_____

_____

_____

_____

_____

_____

_____

_____

_____

_____

_____ (words)

500-WORD ESSAY IN 60 MINUTES

Start Time: _____   End Time: _____

Suggest means to step up education in your city or town.

_____

_____

_____

_____

_____

_____

_____

_____

_____

_____

_____

_____

_____

_____

_____

_____

_____

_____

_____

_____

_____

_____
_____
_____
_____
_____
_____
_____
_____
_____
_____
_____
_____
_____
_____
_____
_____
_____
_____
_____
_____
_____
_____
_____
_____ (words)

500-WORD ESSAY IN 60 MINUTES

Start Time: _____   End Time: _____

Define politics and its role in governing a nation.

_____

_____

_____

_____

_____

_____

_____

_____

_____

_____

_____

_____

_____

_____

_____

_____

_____

_____

_____

_____

_____

_____

_____

_____

_____

_____

_____

_____

_____

_____

_____

_____

_____

_____

_____

_____

_____

_____

_____

_____

_____

_____

_____

_____

_____(words)

CHAPTER 8

ESSAY WRITING
SUMMARY
FORMULA

Fewer Mistakes, Greater Confidence!

Most articles in magazines, journals and newspapers contain the following:

- Repeated / Repetitive information
- Descriptive Language
- Obvious and unnecessary expressions

They are to be crossed out or omitted. The rest of the content is then rearranged and combined to form the summary. This reduces the need to rephrase which is a challenge for many especially those with limited understanding of English.

FORMULA: Summary

The Text / Passage – (Examples + Repetitive Words + Descriptive Words + Phrases with the same or similar meanings + Lengthy Expressions) + Conjunctions and/or Connecting Words

REPETITIVE INFORMATION

Repetitive information is a word or group of words that is the same or different but which expresses the same or similar meaning. Note the example given.

Those are the things that people throw away. They are obviously rubbish.

Explanation: Things that people throw away are rubbish. Thus, both sentences express the same meaning. Which should you cross out? Omit the longer phrase or sentence which is less obvious in conveying the meaning.

~~Those are the things that people throw away.~~ They are obviously rubbish.

So the remaining sentence is the summary. Here is another example.

The headmaster was very angry. He was too angry at the meeting. He decided to discontinue the meeting.

Explanation:
- The words *angry* and *meeting* are repeated, and
- The words *very* and *too* have the same meaning.

The headmaster ~~was very angry. He~~ was too angry ~~at the meeting~~. He decided to discontinue the meeting.

Must remember!

Students are encouraged to combine sentences with either conjunctions or connecting words. Note the example given.

The headmaster was too angry **that** he decided to discontinue the meeting.

Students are also encouraged to change some of the words with words of similar meanings. Note the example given.

The headmaster was **so furious** that he decided to **end** the meeting.

PRACTICE

Identify the repetitive information and combine the sentences with a conjunction or connecting word where necessary.

1. We were arguing. We were not getting along at all.

   _____

2. The engineer was over the moon with his promotion. He was so happy that nothing could bring him down. He decided to celebrate his promotion with a drink.

   _____

   _____

3. I was thrilled. I had never been on a cruise before. I could hardly wait for the day to pass.

   _____

4. A mother will often put her child's safety and wellbeing first before hers. There was once a kid who was crossing a road oblivious to a speeding car. His mother seeing what would happen, ran towards her son, and pushed him hard to the side of the road. Sadly, she was hit.

   _____

   _____

5. The refugee was terrified. He panicked and did not know what to do. He fidgeted all the time and was walking aimlessly in the jungle.

   _____

   _____

6. Reading brings about a lot of benefits. Many things are learnt through reading from survival skills to technological troubleshooting.

   _____

DESCRIPTIVE LANGUAGE

Descriptive language often refers to adjectives and adverbs and other descriptive expressions. Basically, an adjective is a word which describes a noun, and an adverb is a word which describes a verb. An adverb normally ends with 'ly'. Note the example given.

The big magnificent female eagle lands gently on her nest and meticulously feeds her newly-hatched young.

Explanation:
- The adjectives are **big, magnificent, female** and **newly-hatched**.
- The adverbs are **gently** and **meticulously**.

The ~~big magnificent female~~ eagle lands ~~gently~~ on her nest and ~~meticulously~~ feeds her ~~newly-hatched~~ young.

The remaining text is the summary written as follows:

The eagle lands on her nest and feeds her young.

Here is another example.

Little know-it-all Tommy is extremely unpopular in his regular classes which he attends unfailingly. He frequently yaks about his extensive readings and exclusive book collection at home.

Explanation:
- The descriptive words used are **little, know-it-all, extremely, regular, unfailingly, frequently, extensive** and **exclusive**.
- The additional information **which he attends** should also be crossed out.

~~Little know-it-all~~ Tommy is ~~extremely~~ unpopular in his ~~regular~~ classes ~~which he attends~~ ~~unfailingly~~. He ~~frequently~~ yaks about his ~~extensive~~ readings and ~~exclusive~~ book collection at home.

The remaining text is the summary written as follows:

Tommy is unpopular in his classes. He yaks about his readings and book collection at home.

Must remember!

With longer sentences, it is not necessary for students to combine sentences, but to make sentences flow, conjunction or connecting words are still essential. Note the example given.

Tommy is unpopular in his classes **because** he yaks about his readings and book collection at home.

Must remember!

Again, students are encouraged to change some of the words with words of similar meanings. Note the example given.

Tommy is **hated** in his classes because he **babbles** about his readings and book collection at home.

PRACTICE

Identify and omit the descriptive language in the following sentences. Then combine the remaining information with a conjunction or connecting word where necessary.

1. Most young children do not have the mature ability to reason logically. They often make rash decisions based on their personal preferences.

   ----

2. The tiny new born baby, weighing a little over one kilogram in weight, was born prematurely, two months earlier than expected.

   ----

3. She is a compulsive liar who constantly boasts about her extensive achievements in the past. Naturally, there is no solid proof of any of her supposed great work.

   ----

4. In many cases, those who do not hold any strong personal life principles are hypocrites at best. They have multiple characters to suit any situation and people. They simply give wonderful promises that they do not intend to keep.

   ----

5. The typical domestic pets like cats, dogs and fish are wonderful additions to a small family. They can be good and valuable stress relievers.

LENGTHY EXPRESSION

A lengthy expression refers to additional and unnecessary information. Note the example given.

Cellphones are useful things for people to own in this world.

Explanation: The additional information of ***thing for people to own in this world*** is unnecessary as it is obvious that only humans own cellphones. Thus, the remaining text is written as follows:

Summary:
Cellphones are useful.

Here is another example.

Many modern men stay at home on weekday evenings and help out with household chores. Some share the responsibility of taking care of their young children with their wives.

The additional information is crossed out as follows:

~~Many~~ modern men stay at home on weekday evenings and help out with ~~household~~ chores. Some share the responsibility of taking care of their ~~young~~ children ~~with their wives.~~

The remaining text is written as follows:

Summary:
Modern men stay at home on weekday evenings and help out with chores. Some share the responsibility of taking care of their children.

Must remember!

With longer sentences, it is not necessary for students to combine sentences, but to make sentences flow, a conjunction or connecting word is still essential. Note the example given.

Modern men stay at home on weekday evenings and help out with chores **while** others share the responsibility of taking care of their children.

Must remember!

Again, students are encouraged to change some of the words with words of similar meanings. Note the example given.

Modern men stay at home on weekday evenings and help out with **tasks** while others share the responsibility of **looking after** their children.

PRACTICE

Identify and omit the lengthy expressions in the following sentences. Then combine the remaining information with a conjunction or connecting word where necessary.

1. It is hard to find a decent job that pays well in a global downturn where unemployment rate increases and prices of goods fluctuate.

   _____

2. Nothing is free in this life. Everything comes with a price tag. You even have to pay tax on your own property.

   _____

3. It may cost you more to have dinner in a fancy restaurant in the city. Besides the service tax, you pay for the ambiance.

   _____

4. Every nation on earth is made up of different races and ethnic groups. Each has its very own distinct culture and customs.

   _____

5. In the past, many wild animals lived in vast thick jungles in Africa and the Amazon, especially in areas far from human dwellings.

   _____

6. Her cocktail dress, which was perfect for a cocktail party, was orange in colour.

   _____

7. Most real natural flowers smell wonderfully aromatic and are beautiful to look at particularly when they blossom.

   _____

PRACTICE

Summarizing longer passages

EXERCISE 1

Read and summarise the following article. Remember to apply the formula learnt.

DURIAN GALLERY

Durian Gallery is a delightful mini art and décor shop which sells beautiful art work from vintage to abstract and other unique gifts superb for contemporary homes. The interior design of the shop is simple but elegant with a variety of meaningful modern paintings adorning the walls.

The shop owner is a bubbly young lady who came up with the idea of a mini art and décor shop when she was hunting for good paintings to decorate her twin sister's new home.

"It was difficult to get unique and inspiring décor in town. Of course there are a lot of those expensive ones, but I was interested in getting quality décor that was affordable," explained Hasdayana. "So with the support of my family and friends, I set up this gallery in February."

To fully appreciate the décor offered at the shop, one has to visit the gallery at Bandar IJM, which is visible on the right when entering the main road into Bandar IJM. Since its opening, many of its limited edition art décor and gifts have been sold. According to Hasdayana, the art prints offered are not only great wall adornments, but they are also great house warming, business opening and birthday gifts.

Durian is a popular fruit in East Asia and it is very much sort after when in season, but it is not a name that one would have for a shop particularly an art and gift gallery.

"The name of the gallery came with an interesting story. But to make it short, a relative of mine suggested durian because we were durian fanatics, and it was authentically local. I was hesitant at first because customers may think that the shop sells fruits. But then she mentioned the International Apple brand established by the late Steve Jobs and the rest was history."

The shop is opened every day from 10am. In addition to the wall décors, Durian Gallery offers Islamic calligraphy crafts, handmade Indonesian table cloths and curtains, fancy clocks and whacky door signs suitable for homes and offices.

SUMMARY: DURIAN GALLERY

Read and summarise the following article. Remember to apply the formula learnt.

COURSES TAYLORED TO YOUR NEEDS AND BUDGET

There comes a time in many parents' lives when choosing the right courses for their children within the budget becomes a nightmare. Ask any college and university and each one often claims that they are better than the others.

It is practically easy to find out which is the best in their respective fields. Just type 'Best Universities in the World' online and you are presented with a list of the top 100.

Then comes the question: How many can afford the top 100? It is really not about going to the best colleges and universities, but it is about learning all you can and do the best at what you study. After all, there are those who study at top institutions and still fail, and there are also many high income earners who did not graduate from such institutions.

RJ Education Services, a leading education consultant agency recommends that parents and high school graduates first search through the list of courses available online or within their own country and then choose the courses which suit or are within their interests before selecting the colleges or universities. Interest plays an important part in excelling in one's studies. Unfortunately, there is an increasing number of graduates who are working in industries which are not at all related to their field of studies or qualifications. Realistically, the time and money spent on studying the initial courses are just wasted.

Another factor to consider is the courses that attract the most income in the future. Sadly, many parents and students have this idea that common careers like accounting, law, medicine, etc. are the only few which potentially offer handsome income. There are hordes of other careers which offer similar, if not, better pay.

"I have a friend who is working in the hospitality field and she is earning a minimum of eight thousand dollars a month. Her job is tough but it is her interest which drives her to the top and that makes a big difference," commented Joanne, the manager of RJ Education Services. Other careers which also offer high salary are dentistry, advertising and marketing, actuary, engineering, aviation and air traffic controls, management, education administration and teaching, physiotherapy, etc.

Once the courses are selected, the next step is to find the right colleges and universities which offer affordable quality education.

SUMMARY: COURSES TAYLORED TO YOUR NEEDS AND BUDGET

Read and summarise the following article. Remember to apply the formula learnt.

THE TREASURE SHOP

The Treasure Shop is a secondhand shop that was set up by volunteers headed by one of the Sandakan Cheshire Home committee members, Mahsan and her humanitarian friends Tay, Haseley, Kulos, Voon and other volunteers. The shop was set up within a two-month period and was officially opened by one of the State Assemblymen on 15th April 2012.

"We sell secondhand items such as clothing, books, toys, furniture and handmade crafts. All secondhand items donated are preselected to ensure that items sold are of good quality and at affordable prices," informed Kimin, the Cheshire Home supervisor.

The objectives of the Treasure Shop are to provide employment and equal opportunities for persons with disabilities in gaining independent living, create awareness on disability issues and generate income for the Home.

With the full support of the Cheshire Home management and Home Affairs officer, Chu and the generous donations from other non-government organisations, corporations, schools and the general public, the shop earned more than 2000 ringgit in sales in its first week of operation.

Chong, the committee member in charge of overseeing the Treasure Shop added, "Running a non-government organisation such as this is never easy. We are often short of funds and have to unfortunately resort to public donations. One can only ask so much but with this venture, we hope to ease the burden of all our dedicated committee members and volunteers."

The Treasure Shop welcomes secondhand goods and/or hand-me-downs such as clothing, books, toys, furniture, handmade crafts, etc. Donations can be dropped off between 9am and 4pm at the Home located within the vicinity of the old folks home, and at the Home stall at the night market every Saturday from 5pm to 9pm. Pick up can also be arranged for large items. Call 089 631716 for pickup service.

The Treasure Shop is wholly owned by The Sabah Cheshire Home which provides care and shelter for persons with disabilities. The Home in Sandakan was established on 8th April 2000, with the vision to create an enabling environment for persons with disabilities to exercise their rights to lead lives as normal as possible within their capabilities.

SUMMARY: THE TREASURE SHOP

SUMMARY

FORMULA

- **Summary**
  The Text/Passage – (Examples + Repetitive Words + Descriptive Words + Phrases with the same or similar meanings + Lengthy Expressions) + Conjunctions and/or Connecting Words

Must remember!

Tertiary students often have to go through several references when doing research. To save time, identify the content, limiting word(s) and D-word, and find books, articles, etc. relating to them. Browse through the specific or related chapters and find specific information relevant. Once you determine the specific information, start summarising with the formula learnt. Finding the right information should not take you more than an hour or two. More than that, you have a problem. All the best!

ESSAY WRITING

QUESTIONS & TOPICS ON CURRENT ISSUES

Fewer Mistakes, Greater Confidence!

Practise writing an essay at least three times a month. Here are some essay questions and topics on current issues.

1. In general, people are living longer mow. Consider the causes of this phenomenon.

2. Are electoral reforms necessary in your country?

3. What do you see as the greatest threat to the environment today?

4. Discuss the characteristics of a successful leader.

5. Define business ethics.

6. How has the media affected body image?

7. False media report is a growing epidemic.

8. Describe some of today's advertising tactics.

9. What is your view of abusive parents?

10. Consider the vital things a child should be taught.

11. Freedom of speech means the freedom to insult and condemn. Discuss.

12. Compare the ways businesses are run in your country and a neighboring country.

13. Consider the case for a justified war.

14. Is censorship necessary in the media?

15. Think about the taboo in hiring a surrogate mother.

16. What would the world be like without religion?

17. Describe the characteristics of those who do all the talking but take no action.

18. Explain the benefits of education.

19. Write an analysis of the pirates of Silicon Valley.

20. Consider the case for and against euthanasia.

21. Why is public speaking daunting?

22. Discuss the advantages and disadvantages of modern technology.

23. Describe a hacker's life.

24. Think about changing values and culture shock.

25. Suggest ways to manage diversity in the workplace.

26. A bird in hand is worth two in the bush.

27. Globalization is a disadvantage to third world countries. Discuss.

28. How should cases of violence in sports be handled?

29. Is having fear good or bad?

30. Discuss the development of immigration policy in your country.

31. Dowry: a custom or a crime?

32. Consider our shrinking water supply.

33. What are the reasons for the popularity of reality TV?

34. The entertainment industry.

35. "You cannot please all of the people all of the time, so to be fair we should try to please no one." Do you agree?

36. Is passionate conviction sufficient for justifying knowledge?

37. Consider advertising as the catalyst for materialism.

38. Amusing ourselves to death.

39. Discuss the significance of marriage today.

40. What are the causes of World War II?

41. Give an overview of the mentally challenged.

42. Consider the rise in celebrity infatuation.

43. What is your opinion of middle aged entertainers?

44. Choose a controversial problem in college and suggest a solution.

45. State the case for and against the use of cellphones while driving.

46. What do you consider to be the most important social problem? Give reasons.

47. Explain the relation between digital communication and public relation.

48. The climate is changing, and the changes are a threat. How can businesses make positive contributions to the fight against climate change?

49. Why is capitalism so predominant in the global economy?

50. Soccer: The most popular sport in the world.

ESSAY WRITING
ANSWERS
Fewer Mistakes, Greater Confidence!

Identifying a complete sentence

Sentences	Complete / Incomplete
Cooking a new dish.	Incomplete
Is easy.	Incomplete
A vacation will do you a lot of good.	Complete
Sky surfing very exciting.	Incomplete
I will take.	Incomplete
Think about your past.	Complete
Lots of bubbles.	Incomplete
Abel speaks more than one language.	Complete
She often gets irritated.	Complete
Changing a habit can be frustrating.	Complete
Citizens from every state.	Incomplete
To get greater benefit from the government	Complete
The differences between young and old.	Complete
The prime minister can speak in public.	Incomplete
You will perform.	Complete

Rearranging the structure

1. She drives her car with speed.

2. I often go to the supermarket.

3. She paid too much money.

4. The new student has some personal problems with Chinese.

5. It is often difficult to understand Scottish.

6. The emcee spoke English very fast.

7. Do you prefer Korean or Japanese food?

8. He is very good at sweet talking!

9. I have never met Aubrey.

10. Are you the principal or the teacher?

EDITING 1

Many companies in Malaysia offer job vacancies from general clerks to plantation managers. Unfortunately, many are often rejected due to their monolingual proficiency.

Broken language is not acceptable at work. With many companies investing overseas and merging with foreign companies, knowing only one language puts one at the end of the employment queue. While science and mathematics are important, communication in general is not expressed in formulas and numbers.

They say charity begins at home and so does education. Many parents forget that in many cases, success comes through hardship. It is not uncommon for parents especially in South East Asia to support their young adult children. And it is also common that many parents withdraw their kids from academic courses when they seem tough.

Thus, this gives rise to a monolingual society because when learning one or two more languages seems impossible, abandonments follow. When learning becomes impossible, there is no hope for the future. Some opinions may differ but this fact remains, unless a person is medically classified mentally challenged, stupidity does not exist. On the other hand, laziness is nurtured from young.

EDITING 2

Set up in 1989, Alice's restaurant is famous for its tasty steamed buns, soupy dim sums, traditional cakes, Hainanese chicken rice and spicy tom yam. It is a family business run by a Muslim couple, so 'halal' food is guaranteed.

There are two key words given priority at Alice's: Quality and Cleanliness. They are very much part of Alice's formula to a long running business.

Located in the heart of Kim Fung town, the ambience at Alice's remains the same except for a few wall decorations and the grade A certificates awarded by the Ministry of Health approving the overall cleanliness of the restaurant. Many regulars feel very much at home at Alice's.

Alice, the manager, learnt the art of culinary from foreign chefs and bakers, but also from those whose creations came straight from their home kitchens. Having at least two decades of cooking experience in culinary science and the sheer love for cooking, Alice is a master of modification and until today, her modified recipes remain a secret.

Already in their 70s, Alice and Mahsan still run their business with the assistance of their children. They are friendly and are accustomed to having a good chat with customers.

EDITING 3

In 2010, I signed on the dotted line and joined the Toastmasters Club. It took me 2 years to conjure up the courage to put myself in the spotlight and speak in public. I experienced everything a virgin public speaker would usually go through. I had sweaty palms, palpitations, butterflies, etc. Fortunately, I did not wet my pants.

Speaking in public is no doubt a harrowing ordeal but once the skills are mastered and the fidgeting controlled, the door of opportunity opens naturally. Public speaking is an important part of communication which does not only expand a person's social and professional networks, but it also leads to a better career and life quality.

Toastmasters' meetings are never short of laughter too. People get kicks out of presenting humorous speeches and the audience gets to relax and enjoy their evenings with some wholesome entertainment. In addition, Toastmasters put fun in learning. Members are allowed to make mistakes and the more presentations made, the more a person improves particularly in body language and vocal variety.

I never regretted my decision to join the club. My speaking skills are more refined and my confidence is superb. Put me in front of a thousand people and I guarantee that my palms remain dry, the butterflies and palpitations cease to exist and my pants are zipped, and I am ready for action.

Identify and underline the Content word(s)

1. Define '<u>beauty</u>' and describe how beauty is perceived today.

2. The advantages and disadvantages of <u>freedom of speech</u>.

3. '<u>Money</u> is not everything.' Do you agree?

4. Is <u>killing</u> ever justified?

5. '<u>Being an entertainer</u> is not all glitzy.' What do you think?

6. Why is it difficult to learn a new <u>language</u>?

7. What is your view of <u>military service</u> being made obligatory?

8. To what extent is <u>home schooling</u> effective?

9. Describe <u>the activities of religious people</u> in your country.

10. Discuss the case for and against <u>gay marriages</u>.

Identify and underline the Limiting word(s)

1. Is population control <u>necessary in China</u>?

2. How popular is KPOP <u>in your country</u>?

3. Discuss <u>the advantages and disadvantages</u> of YouTube.

4. Consider <u>the practical measures in controlling an outbreak</u> such as H7N9.

5. Should politics <u>be taught in secondary or high school</u>?

6. Children are sometimes demanding. <u>To what extent should parents follow their demands?</u>

7. Do entrepreneurs <u>go for status upgrade or financial promotions</u>?

8. Is it <u>practical to have singing and dancing</u> as part of co-curricular activities?

9. What is your view of <u>an honest</u> business <u>person</u>?

10. Do you think <u>it is possible to live without</u> the internet today?

Repetitive Information

1. We were arguing.
2. The engineer was so happy that he decided to celebrate with a drink.
3. I was thrilled as I had never been on a cruise before.
4. A mother would often put her child's safety and wellbeing first before hers.
5. The refugee was terrified and did not know what to do.
6. Reading brings about a lot of benefits.

Descriptive Language

1. Children do not have the ability to reason. They make decisions based on their preferences.
2. The baby was born two months early.
3. She is a liar who boasts about her past achievements / achievements in the past.
4. Those do not hold life principles are hypocrites. They do not keep promises / They give promises they do not keep.
5. Pets are wonderful additions to a family. They can be stress relievers.

Lengthy Expression

1. It is hard to find a job in a global downturn.
2. Nothing is free.
3. It costs more to have dinner in a restaurant in the city.
4. Every nation is different.
5. In the past, many animals lived in jungles.
6. Her cocktail dress was orange.
7. Most flowers are aromatic and beautiful.

About Author

Cindy Mahsan is a freelance advertiser, writer and an experienced teacher who has worked in Malaysia and Singapore. She is the editor of Passing Time Newsletter, a free advertising publication, and she teaches English literature and psychology at a leading university in Malaysia.